# Mapping Home

a collection of poems

Savita Krishnamoorthy

Arjun Nagamangalam

for aakriti
our ray of sunshine
always in our hearts!

It's only by stopping movement that you can see where to go.

~Pico Iyer

# Table of Contents

where i am from

# where i am from – 1

## Arjun (12)


i am from books crammed into shelves, from dog toys and chewed
up socks
i am from pots filled with flowers, and from my dog scampering
around our backyard
i'm from the short, stout bushes and the towering pines, swaying in
the breeze
i am from my birthdays, and mom and dad
i am from piano when it fills the house with music
i'm from my grandparents, and cards
i am from, "get off the computer!" and all sorts of indian dishes
i am from my hammock in between the trees
i'm from my bike, riding to the bike park and doing jumps
i am from all the memories in my mind
and many more to come

# a forest

Arjun (14)

surrounded by dark green

with flashes of color here and there

the chirping of the birds is everywhere

they tweet and chirrup for joy

the gentle crunch of the ground beneath your feet

and the trees whisper above you

"wisha wisha wisha"

# mount rainier

### Arjun (13)

mount rainier was a precise assignment

our noble guide, connor, led us endless

he taught us about the changing climate

and what we can do to stop the process(es)


we were a collection of blackberries

searching for how the forest would burn down

we took results with a few adversaries

and presented our info back at town


the squadron summited the great mountain

where some of us went farther than others

soon, we were craving a water fountain

but we found none from the great earth mother


mount rainier was quite a great adventure

and we were blessed with adequate weather

# constellations

## Arjun (13)

the sun slowly falls off the sky
getting ready to sleep through the night
meanwhile the moon wakes up
preparing for its day

the moon calls to the stars
calls for them to come out
the stars gently show their faces
to see what the moon is calling them for

the moon corrals them into their shapes
turning them into constellations
glowing and shimmering in the night sky
the stars smile upon the earth

the night soon comes to a close
the moon has finished its work
the stars go back to sleep
and the sun will soon emerge

# spring poem 1

### Arjun (14)

pale green buds sprouting
blossoming into petals of blood
thorny teeth always surrounding
it is but a rose

# the ocean

Arjun (8)

the ocean is like

    the setting sun

    a fun playground

    an animal on the hunt

    a long journey

    a faraway planet

# the crow

Arjun (13)

a shadow flying in the sky
feathers black as coal
a call - feels like a scream
caw, caw, caw
he soars across the world

# spring poem 2

Arjun (14)

inspired by Shi Jing


how the cherry blossoms bloom
as far as the eye can see!
a sparrow perched amongst them
hiding away from the inky rain

how the cherry blossoms bloom
as far as the eye can see!
laying beneath the broad boughs
a soft breeze washes over me
crisp spring air all around

bathed by delicate sunshine
the cherry trees are empty
flowers on the ground
the rain begins to drift away
soon, summer will come

# the peacock

Arjun (13)


a flash of blue

in the dark green forest

its hundred eyes gazing upon you

its majestic tail unfurled

as quick as it appeared, it is gone

# where i am from - 2

Arjun (14)

i am from books, from fresh fruit, and nature

i'm from music, from the chromatic black and white of the piano

the singing of the instrument as it tells a story that words never could

from bach, and beethoven, chopin, and liszt

i am from india, in nashik, and bangalore

from hinduism, and monasteries in the mountains of the himalayas

from the million and one different gods and goddesses

i am from travel, from spain to sweden

from exploring new places, exotic cultures

unfamiliar foods and delicious new tastes

sweet, creamy, rasmalai, and fresh, savory seafood from as early as i

can remember

the sugary crackle of buttery-smooth crème brûlée and the bitter

richness of tiramisu

the spiciness of thai curries, and the delicious satisfying warmth of a

hot pot

i am from the crisp, cool air of autumn mornings, from the vivid

hues of red and yellow

from sports and the outdoors

i'm from the fresh morning air in the middle of the forest,

surrounded by the chirping of birds and the trickle of a stream

gazing upon a deep orange sky as the sun sets on us, ready to go to

sleep

mountain, mother

# the silent sentinel

### Savita

colossal

majestic

towering

imperial


you exude

a powerful presence

spiritual splendor

the abode of shiva


sunlight caresses your crown

you shimmer

in jewel tone colors

like a luminous, glowing bride


blazing blues

pristine purples

radiant reds

opulent oranges


you embody

protection

sanctuary

refuge


you are

a silent sentinel

a solitary spirit

a sacrosanct soul

# happy 70th amma!

Savita

she has good cheer aplenty
a thousand-watt smile
an eternal optimism that
never ceases for even a little while

she can truly have a belly laugh
tears streaming down her face
laughing at things inconsequential
trying hard to maintain decorum and grace

an insatiable zest for learning
discovering the joys of the world
with a curiosity and childlike wonder
watching it all unfurl

you want her in your corner
when the chips are down
a backbone made of steel
handling it all with nary a frown

a confidant, a mentor, a friend
to countless people, age no bar
they all remember her fondly
some near, many others from afar

the guiding light in our lives
aim for the stars and beyond the sky
this is what you always taught us
live life with your head held high

carnival

# the miracle of crème brûlée

Arjun (13)


a gallon of cream goes into the pot
gently simmering and bubbling
a sack of sugar follows it in
and soon, a drop of vanilla

a dozen egg yolks are whisked for a day
then the cream is added drop by drop
for another two weeks it is whisked
until all is together

the concoction is poured into cups
the cups put into the oven
and left to sit
for three days

once they have baked
they must be retrieved
and left to cool
until they are cold as ice

the set custards have one final transformation
a spoon of sugar is sprinkled over top
the custards are blasted
with the heat of the sun

all this work
for a lovely dessert

# best friend

### Arjun (13)

he awakes early in the morning
ready to explore what the day has ahead of him
his bushy tail follows him everywhere
wagging back and forth

on walks, he is curious
sniffing and searching for whatever he can find
always joyous, never sad
constantly living his best life

in the afternoons, he is sleepy
he gently and peacefully naps
curled up into a ball of fluff
he dozes away

the evening is his favorite
his tail wagging rapidly
like a fan, it emits a breeze
as it goes from side to side

soon, his day is over
he sprawls himself over the cool hardwood floor
happily, he snoozes the night away
my golden friend, copper!

# the piano

Arjun (13)


the piano can be as bright as the brightest star
shining against the midnight sky
or as dark as a charcoal pencil
like a black silhouette against a white background

the piano can be as fierce as a lion
low and proud
but it can be as graceful as a butterfly
with sound fluttering in ripples and shimmers

the piano can be like a water lily
floating on a lake of music
with each note so clearly etched
on a sea of black and white

the piano sounds like a carnival
with colors left and right
like a rainbow
over the light blue sky

the piano can be as wide as a ballroom
with your fingertips as the dancers
back and forth they go
waltzing until the very end

# elegy to a coffee truck

Arjun (15)


a glorious arrival blesses the school
students flocking to drink it all up
the greatest gift in the time of yule
when coffee is given in peoples' cup

in the eighth hour the barista begins
churning out pint after pint of drink
the awaiting line of freshmen with grins
appears to have absolutely no shrink.

at last, my turn is here
the cold has made me sore
i request my order, but without any cheer
he declares "the cappuccino is no more."

oh! the twangs of pain strike deep!
the sole drink that i needed
taken from me, makes me want to weep
for the coffee, my soul pleaded

# cards

## Arjun (12)

a deck of cards are fifty-two paintings
each one so delicately crafted
so carefully painted
fifty-two times

a deck of cards is endless fun
with so many games
and countless hours spent
playing and playing

a deck of cards is a kingdom
a hierarchy
with the king and queen at the top
the jack below the king and queen
and all the numbers beneath the jack

a deck of cards is a storybook
each card tells a different tale
and together they make a saga
within their paper walls

# panna cotta

## Arjun (14)

a simple dessert

yet so delicious

a rich, decadent dessert of cream

the scent of subtle bourbon and sweet vanilla fills the room

a gentle wobble as it makes its way toward you

sailing on its spoon

# procrastination

Arjun (14)

i am so lazy i think i will procrastinate later!

~ Arjun (10)


a laziness

void of productivity

it gives me a little sadness

that there's almost no activity


nothing is happening

but the time flies by quickly

it feels like i'm a mannequin

just sitting there quietly


my time has run out

my homework needs validation

but i have nothing to show for it

because of my procrastination

aakriti

# aakriti

Savita

you came into our lives
full of hope and light
we thought you
would always be within sight

when I look up at the sky
i see you shine bright
the most dazzling star
in the still, dark night

though your time with us
was brief on earth
you live forever
in our hearts and in our hearth

# gossamer

## Savita

frantic hands
worried faces
anxious voices

like an explosion of thunder, shattering the bedlam
mercurial as lightning
you arrived

unexpected
sudden
too soon…too soon

i was sucked into a maelstrom
of tubes, monitors, needles, and ventilators
suffocating my senses, my spirit, my soul

through a haze of fog and mist
a rare ray of sunshine
timidly peeking, hesitant, diffident

offering an illusory hope
lulling us into a utopian delusion
daring us to dream

then like the gossamer wings of a butterfly
you floated away
slowly, so excruciatingly slowly

into eternity

timelessness

too soon…too soon

# my sister

Arjun (13)

imagine, for a second
a sister you never knew
a friend you never saw
someone so close
yet only seen in photos
i would often find myself wondering
"what would she have been like?"

march 26, 2005
she was brought into this world
from the very beginning it was suffering
congenital diaphragmatic hernia was the name of her condition
she had a hole in her diaphragm
she could not breathe!

for almost four months she was constrained to the hospital
like an inmate in a prison
but it was the only way she could live
she came home for two weeks
oxygen tanks with her to keep her alive
tubes through her nose to get air into her
blankets to keep her from freezing as cold as ice
but she was safe
she was safe....

or so my parents thought
precautions on top of precautions failed

her lungs could not support her

rushing to the hospital in a blur for a chance, just one more chance to

save her!

she never had a chance to live!

july 20, 2005

she was gone!

# ground zero

### Savita


sound

the rustling rasp of scissors slashing through fabric in a frenzied rush

slicing precisely down the middle, like there was an invisible ruler

separating forever the two pink bunnies

that had hitherto been linked on the front of a yellow t-shirt

not a bright sunny yellow, a more mellow yellow

a yellow like the underside of a pat of butter

the fancy kind you get in a fancy restaurant

the humming of monitors, the hush of anxious voices, the beeping of machines

harried feet shuffling silently on the linoleum floor

the sound of anguish!


sight

big brown eyes searching in confusion and fear

begging to be taken back into the comfort of familiar arms

away from the prodding, poking, and prying

not be abandoned on the cold, metallic hospital table

because this would be the point of no return


taste

bitter coffee mixed with the faint acrid taste of aspirin

coating the back of the throat

the sourness in the mouth, sharp and biting

the coiling dread in the pit of the stomach

brought on by anxiety and a suffocating fear of the unknown

smell

the sharp astringent of antiseptic

purell, clorox, dettol

sanitizing the hands, varnishing the floor, cleansing the body

juxtaposed with the faint odor of the remains of a sandwich

and the sickening whiff of stale fries

forlorn, forgotten, and congealed in their crumpled oil-stained paper

bag

discarded by unknown worried hands tearing the fraying edges into

tassels


touch

a tiny body swaddled in the softest of blankets

it should have been warm because of the many layers

but it is cold, so cold like it was frozen

frozen like my heart is at this moment

watching the numbers dropping on the monitor

my heart plummeting in unison with those on the screen

touching ground zero and my world stopping

where time and space fuse and the air around

morphs into a languid, liquid state

i am underwater, sinking deep into an abyss

a cocooning numbness that i don't want to emerge from


silence

haunts most of all!

# pink dress

Savita

a tiny pink and white checkered dress
really more fit for a doll
but then you were not much bigger
all of two pounds
so eager to come into this world

fighting for four months
before
giving up with a tired sigh
and sleeping now for all eternity

i am afraid
to open this box of memories
where they lie
all carefully wrapped and cocooned
cushioned against the wrinkles of life

i want to hold on to the scent of you
the fragrance tucked into the folds of your pink dress
faint wisps of baby powder
and cleansing soap

the memories are getting more elusive
as time goes by
like trying to catch
a sunbeam in the palm of your hand

the harder you try
the faster it escapes
like powdered sugar through a sieve
fleeting, transient, ephemeral

i am judicious in what i remove today
carefully choosing one
peeling it off
layer by layer
moment by moment

like a child prudently choosing a favorite candy
i take one out slowly
to cherish and treasure
freezing a frame in my consciousness

until it is time
to put it back again
into my repository of reminiscences
and hope that the memory remains
vivid and clear
the next time it is unwrapped

pearl, dipped

(Savita)

memories rest undisturbed within the pages yellowing with age, creased, and crinkled.

they remind me of my father's hands, also wrinkled and weathered with the patina of a lifetime.

the skin stretched over the knuckles to an almost papery thin, fragile texture.

much like the pages themselves.

september is a cusp, on the edge of summer but not yet ready to take the leap into the fall. she is wedged between the bright yellows and brilliant greens of the preceding warm months, and the mellow honeyed oranges and glowing titian reds of those to follow.

i remind myself to shed my anxieties, fears, self-doubts. to take a pause from time to time, and rest/rejuvenate/restore/my physical, emotional, and spiritual spirit.

to (re)imagine and (re)kindle my hopes and dreams.

the days will get shorter, the sunshine softer, its golden fingers enveloping like a warm, fuzzy blanket.

early mornings will start to get misty and foggy, all soft blues, greys.

and every so often, an elusive purple making the mountains outside look like a hokusai woodcut.

the light is like the glow of a pearl that is dipped in the softest of iridescent hues – luminous and ephemeral. you breathe too hard, and it will float away.

so, it is best to be silent. inhale with slow, measured breaths, and hope that just for a moment, time stands still.

the horizon is low. the sky dominates the space.

there are fields and fields of lupins in all their untamed glory, growing abundantly, exploding in a sea of amethyst.

they create a lavender haze when seen from a distance, especially whilst encircling a mountain.

memories scattered across geographies

where/what is home?

where i am going

# gratitude

Savita

the earth took a deep cleansing breath
and let out a grateful sigh
peeling off the layers of trauma
of years of abuse and neglect
mapped on the skin of her lands
in the bones of her mountains
and the undulations of her hills
in the dimples of her valleys
and in the silken depths of her oceans
this collective trauma that is transcending
borders and boundaries
cultures and communities
politics and philosophies

the bees are finally back
dancing in the dappled sunlight
that pours over the blueberry bush
like molten, amber honey
the straggling weeds are deliriously charting
merry new paths in my garden where
the dog scampers happily
blissfully oblivious to
social distancing
6 feet apart
shelter in place
flattening the curve
endemic versus pandemic
our new vocabulary

a layered lexicon

of a multiplicity of meanings


the walks outside have never been more meaningful

the gentle breeze never been so calming

the children's chatter more uplifting

strangers' smiles more welcoming

(i learned the myriad ways that eyes can smile, even through

makeshift masks!)


my positionality is in that nebulous space

in the intersections of gratitude and privilege

as I re/calibrate and unmask dis/comfort

my heart is now getting used to


a new normal!

# we breathe the air

### Arjun (16)

we breathe the air, we gasp and choke
enormous clouds of smog and smoke
for plants and trees, what shall we do?
that life on earth can start anew
before it's far too late

and how to show the world we dream
to heal the shattered woods of green
there's simply nothing else to do
we breathe the air

# Author's Note

A note to the reader that the numbers beside Arjun's name in the poems indicate his age at the time of writing them. I hope it helps you follow the evolving ideas at that period of his life. I have left his words largely untouched except for some minor edits in spelling and formatting to ensure that Arjun's voice remains his own.

My wish for the book is that it takes you on your own singular journey of memories and musings, makes you smile, maybe even laugh out loud, reflect, and ultimately celebrate life in its ordinary, and not-so-ordinary moments.

Savita

September 20, 2021

# Acknowledgments

Writing for me is mostly a solitary practice, but so many fill my heart, nourish my spirit, hold my hand, and always stand by me when I do what I love.

My father, T. S. Krishnamoorthy, for gifting me the love of words.

I am indebted to Sati Mookherjee for your care and generosity throughout this journey. For the close reading of my manuscript, your poetic eye, and at the core, our beautiful friendship.

Thank you, Ganesh Anantharaman, and Gauri Shringarpure, for your valuable feedback in the early stage of my curation. You helped me work through the sections with which I was struggling.

My extended family and friends, for your love and steadfast encouragement of my writing.

Sanjay, my biggest cheerleader with the most generous heart. You inspire me to do my best, always.

My sweet boy, Arjun, thank you for allowing me to release your work into the world. You make me laugh. You fill our home with your beautiful piano music. You are the light of my life.